FOR
WE
ARE

FOR WE ARE

Toward Understanding Your Personal Potential

MARK KING
Duquesne University

ADDISON-WESLEY PUBLISHING COMPANY
Reading, Massachusetts · Menlo Park, California
London · Amsterdam · Don Mills, Ontario · Sydney

Second printing, June 1975

 Printed in the United States of America. Published simultaneously in Canada. Library of Congress Catalog Card No. 74-10354.

ISBN 0-201-03747-5
CDEFGHIJ-AL-79

. . . or not to be a clangbird

Photographs

Jeff Schapira

To:

Al and Bernice—who gave me life.

To:

The hundreds of persons who shared themselves with me, and touched me—you are the greatest raw data a scientist could ever have. This book is really about you.

To:

Those beautiful people I call friend—

"You make me meaningful,
Without you I am unendurable (to me).
I will do all I can for you,
To make meaning out of me."

Dave Torbett

To:

My impending death—an awareness of which makes today beautiful.

To:

Snoopy and Judi—who, with a lick and a kiss each morning, remind me that I am alive.

Especially, To:

Judi—For she is.

Contents

For We Are

Chapter One

Who am I and who are you and who are we?
It only matters that we are.
And it doesn't matter if we are today or tomorrow
or yesterday, because we can't be never—we are.
And being what we are, I can't promise you tomorrow—
for I am only promised today.
So let this be my commitment:
Now I will love you in all the ways I can love.
And we'll both have to have faith in tomorrow.
But in case tomorrow is not yours or mine, let me
Grow from you today.
For we are.

What and Why

Chapter Two

This book is about mental health. Before beginning to write, I asked many people—college students, other adults, and even children—to define mental health. Most people defined mental health as mental illness, with a notation that health is simply an absence of pathology. When asked if this definition left room to consider that some people might be healthier than most others, those replying generally dealt with the idea that "normal" people have a "normal" amount of neurotic symptoms (hang-ups) and that healthier persons have fewer of these "hang-ups" than do most others. It is this pervasive cultural assumption—that mental health is simply and only an absence of psychological pathology— that motivated me to write this book. I believe that this assumption is as false as some of our other cultural myths, e.g., masturbation is bad for a person, daydreaming is a sign of discontent or sickness. However, I think that the assumption about mental health is more dangerous than most of our other myths because it directs many people to strive to be normal (not sick) rather than to consider and develop their fullest possible potential—in other words, to go beyond normalcy. This stems partly from our culture's obsession with conformity—being like everyone else. Most of us grow up believing that if we conform (are "normal"), we will be happy and productive and that if we do not conform (are not "normal"), we will be faced with the only other possibility—mental illness of varying forms and degrees.

Such a belief, besides being untrue, is a misuse of the term "normal." The term "normal" (average) is a statistical concept. Its usage usually implies that there are different directions or ways in which we can be something other than normal. Let's use an example most of us are familiar with, the I.Q. test score. On most I.Q. tests, a score of between 90 and 110 is the norm, the range within which most people score. Yet we know that there are two directions in which one can go in order to get an abnormal score—either higher or lower than the normal range. Neither 70 nor 130 is a normal score; both scores are equally abnormal because each score is attained by the same percentage of the population. Yet we do not say that people with these scores are sick because they are not normal. In fact, a score of 130 is highly valued in our culture because it reflects a high intelligence.

If we want to use the concept of normalcy to describe mental health, then we should give to it the statistical properties the term denotes. In the same way that I.Q. scores can vary from normal scores, so too can mental health vary from normalcy. Some of these ways are in a negative direction, which we call mental illness—extreme anxiety, usually an inability to cope with ongoing responsibilities, and in extreme cases a loss of touch with reality. Some of these deviations are in a positive direction and it is this deviation that I am calling mental health.

The term mental health has many value connotations associated with it, so at this point, I would like to give my operational definition of the term.

X	X	X
Mental illness (neither well adjusted nor well developed)	Normalcy (well adjusted)	Mental health (self-actualizing, fully functioning, well developed)

Hypothetically, all people can be ranked on this scale in terms of where they stand relative to their general psychological functioning. (I say "hypothetically" because in reality, no one can validly rank anyone else's psychological functioning; furthermore, because of the ways in which we deceive ourselves, it is even difficult to rank oneself with any accuracy.) Most people would be ranked near the middle of the scale, i.e., normalcy. Some would be ranked, in varying degrees of distance from the center, toward that end labeled mental illness. Others would be ranked toward the other end of the scale, again in varying

degrees of distance from the center. It is this extreme other end of the scale that I am calling mental health and that small percentage of individuals who would be ranked there that I am calling mentally healthy. Abraham Maslow has called these people "self-actuali*zing*" (rather than self-actualiz*ed*) in order to emphasize the notion of continuous growth, and Carl Rogers has described these people as "fully functioning." If you prefer, substitute either of these terms (or one of your own)each time I use the term mental health.

Another way to look at this is in terms of adjustment and development. Adjustment is always seen in terms of a cultural standard of acceptable and nonacceptable behavior. Almost by definition, the majority of people in any society (those falling within the normalcy range of the scale) are seen as well-adjusted individuals. (The only exception to this that I can think of is in a time of great phsyical danger, e.g., an earthquake, when for a short period of time few people seem able to adjust themselves to the situation.) Development is seen in terms of individual potentials—some fairly unique and some shared by many others. A mentally healthy person is one who comes close (no one ever gets completely there) to realizing his or her full potential in many different areas of existence. By this definition, a mentally healthy person is a well-developed person. As will be discussed in detail in Chapter Three, a mentally healthy person is in many ways different from the average person and, therefore, may be seen as not well adjusted. For example, a mentally healthy male may be utilizing his full emotional potential and may therefore sometimes cry in public. A mentally healthy female may need to act very independent in order to actualize her full creative potential. Both of these people may be well-developed individuals, yet may be seen by others as not well adjusted because they do not conform to behavior patterns which our culture prescribes for males and females.

A mentally ill person is like the mentally healthy person in that his or her behavior can often be described as not well adjusted. However, a mentally ill person does not have the personal resources (development) to deal with society's reaction to the lack of adjustment and therefore usually reacts dysfunctionally by becoming extremely anxious, withdrawn, etc. You will note that I am describing the mentally ill person by using such words as "anxiety" and "withdrawn." Although each of us can use these words to describe ourselves at some time in our lives, this does not mean that we are all mentally ill. Rather, the condition that we call mental illness is simply an exaggeration of things that we all feel and ways in which we all behave. Not only the mentally ill and the average, but even the mentally healthy person feels anxious sometimes.

But this book is not about mental illness or pathology. Instead, I am trying to make the distinction between the average person and the healthy person. This distinction—between the average person and the healthy one—may be difficult for you to grasp, because a direct translation of the academic discussion above is simply that most of you reading this book are neither mentally healthy nor mentally ill; you are just average. An analogy may make this distinction clearer. As many of us get older, we let our bodies get out of shape. We eat too much, we don't exercise, we smoke or drink too much, etc. Similarly, most people are not physically sick—they don't need to see a doctor—but they are not as healthy as they could be, either; they're a little too fat, have too many aches and pains, or have slower reflexes than they should for their age. In short, the average person is physically okay—he or she is certainly not sick—but he or she is not in top-notch physical condition. I think that most persons are psychologically okay, too; they're not sick, but yet they're not all that healthy, either.

Most of us, at some time during our lives, realize that we are not physically healthy and strive to improve our condition by dieting, exercising, or seeking aid from a professional (e.g., a medical doctor). The danger of the normal-equals-health equation, in terms of psychological function, is that most of us never realize that we *can* be something better than just normal, and we therefore do not strive for the kind of growth that is possible. Perhaps the greatest advance in American psychology during the past 25 years resulted from the work of the late Abraham Maslow, who demonstrated the value of studying the lives of mentally healthy persons. He suggested that we use these persons as a model, or goal, in examining our own lives and suggested that these healthy people are the "growing edge" of our society.

If you remain open to the material in this book, at the end you might reject my basic idea that the average person is not very healthy. Or, you might agree with me and conclude that you are one of these healthy individuals and react, I suppose, with some satisfaction. The risk you take in having an honest dialogue with this material is that you might agree with me and see yourself as average and thus feel somewhat uncomfortable with yourself. The purpose of this book is not to classify anyone or put anyone down. However, if some of you can use any resulting discomfort as stimulation to examine yourself and your world and maybe make some changes in the direction of growth, then this book will be doing one of the jobs for which it was intended.

What does Chapter One, the poem, have to do with mental health? There are four reasons why I started the book with it. First, it is an example of one person, me, tapping a new area of potential. Until I was 25 years old, I had absolutely no interest in poetry and was positive that I had no potential as a poet. Then, out of a close relationship with a person who communicated through poetry, I found that I had some poetry in me, and through it I learned a new way to communicate my thoughts and feelings. Second, by sharing some of myself rather than quoting from another source or talking academically about people in general, I, hopefully, have demonstrated one of the traits listed in Chapter Three as being important to the mentally healthy person—the ability for self-disclosure. This is sometimes a big problem area for me, but one in which I think I have made progress over the last few years. Third, the message I was trying to express when I wrote the poem has to do with one of the more important traits listed in Chapter Three—time competence, living in the here and now. Fourth, the poem was written during an encounter-group experience, the kind of experience discussed in Chapter Four.

Now that you know what the book is about, is it for you and if so, why should you read it? This book is for students—particularly, but not exclusively, beginning students—in psychology, sociology, child development, human development, and education. It is also for the interested lay person (nonstudent), particularly parents. Some more advanced students may have the background to read more detailed accounts of the self-actualization model (mental health) and, therefore, may find the bibliography at the end of the book more helpful than the ideas in the book itself. I would particularly like to recommend the works of Maslow and Laing, whose names are probably familiar to advanced students, and the work of Ernest Keen (*Psychology and the New Consciousness*), which is probably not familiar to many of you, but which, in my opinion, is an important recent contribution to this area of psychology.

Why do I think it is important that beginning students concern themselves with a model of mental health? I have found that most of the students in the psychology and child development courses I have taught come to class with no real goals in terms of what they want to happen to the people they plan to work with professionally; they have no idea what real potential every person has (this goes back to the "normal is best" model that most of us were raised with). From the philosophical viewpoint of the humanistic school, one can argue that we should not have goals for those we work with, that our goal should be to let each person do his or her own thing. In one sense, I would agree with that; however, I have seen this mode of thought used as an excuse for ignorance. All parents have important, long-lasting effects on their children. Many teachers and psychologists have important influences on the people with whom they come in contact. To neither understand what influences one has nor consider these influences in relation to the potential every person has seems to me to be acting out of ignorance for the sake of a philosophy. Ignorance has never been the best solution to problem-solving or to planning.

As a student, it was somewhat difficult for me to learn psychology, because I had no goal, no view of the nature of people that excited me. Oh, I learned to train rats to press bars in Skinner boxes and to teach pigeons to peck at red rather than green lights, and I also learned all about psychopathology so that I could grow up to be a therapist and save the world (at $25.00 an hour!). But in those years I never learned anything about what a person could become. Now, as a teacher, I find it difficult to teach students who do not have a real goal or purpose. Sure, I can teach students to use behavior-modification principles in order to toilet-train children faster than usual, but so what? What is it leading to? Until one deals with that question, there is no way to "put it all together," to integrate the things one learns in school into a viable, workable action-plan that will be functional to oneself and to those one works with

To put this another way, we cannot decide whether we should walk or take the bus, car, train, or plane until we first decide where we want to go. It is obvious that the decision about how to get somewhere depends partly on what it is we want of that transportation. In the same way, we cannot determine the best method of child rearing without first considering what type of person we want to rear. We cannot decide what methods of education are best until we first decide on the purpose of our educational system. Too often, I have seen the question of method isolated from the question of goal—which, to me, is exactly like deciding on a method of transportation without ever discussing the destination. (I am, of course, making the assumption here that we can all agree that the job of being a parent includes more than just finding the most efficient way to toilet-train the child and that the job of schools goes beyond teaching Sally that 2 + 2 = 4.)

Without making plans for job training, your occupational existence becomes almost totally dependent on chance. In the same way, without making plans about where and how you want to grow psychologically and interpersonally, these areas of existence become totally dependent on chance. To paraphrase the philosopher Nietzsche, we should stop letting our existence be a thoughtless accident.

Before we go on to the model of mental health, there are a few more points I want to discuss briefly. The first is that although I decided to write this book while on a mountain top (in Colorado), I did not carve it on a stone tablet! In other words, I am not asserting that the model of mental health presented here represents any absolute truth about what a healthy person should be. In existential philosophy, there is an important difference between truth and reality. Truth is something that is separate from people, and it usually can't even be identified (I know of no one who can give you the absolute truth about what a mentally healthy person is). For example, the truth is that other planets have more than one moon. But since I am not a scientist dealing in such matters and since I have never experienced the beauty of two or more moons at the same time, this truth has no meaning for me. Reality, on the other hand, is by definition something that is a part of you. It is something that you have experienced, and it is the meaning that you give to that experience. To understand anyone, you need to understand that person's reality. Piaget has shown us that very young children (under one year) do not have the cognitive capacity to understand that when an object leaves their sight, it still exists somewhere else. In order to understand an infant's behavior when its mother leaves, you need to understand how the child sees the situation, not to project your perception of "the truth" of the situation onto the child.

The purpose of this book is to stimulate you, the reader, to consider the potential you have (as do those around you) and to consider it in enough depth so that it becomes part of your reality. *The absolute truth of my model is not important.* Take your reality and expand on it. Throw out the things that have no meaning to you. (Some of my opinions may be the exact opposite of what you feel a healthy person should be.) Add your own traits and values. Read the works of other writers. Most important, enter into a dialogue with the material. Deal with the material at the level of your personal existence—not just your head—and from that dialogue begin to develop your own model of mental health, one that has an important personal meaning for you and one that is functional to you as a person-parent-professional.

Every person has his or her own ideas about mental health—indeed, a personal theory of personality. I cannot see how one can live in the world without making some assumptions about what people are like. Even the most rigid scientist makes many of his or her life's choices and professional decisions on the basis of personal metaphilosophical beliefs. Too often, these beliefs are put down or are denied because they are antiscientific and the "objective observer" has no room for them, which makes about as much sense as saying that the Vietnam war did not exist because, after all, Congress never declared war. If an objective professional is a person with no biases, no preconceived view of people and the world, then I've never met one. If, on the other hand, an objective professional is a person who is willing to consider how his or her results are affected by personal views, if this person is willing to make those views public so that other people can consider the results in light of these values and preconceptions, then we have an objective scientist whose data I can trust or an objective teacher whose lessons I can openly consider.

Every person reading this book has a theory or model of mental health—some goal they are working toward, even if that goal is only to be "normal." Most often, these views remain hidden, covert, because among other things, school teaches you that what you have to say is not important (see Chapter Four) and that your job is to learn the theories of Freud and Skinner and then to pick one to work with. I think it is extremely important that school become a place where students both make their covert theories overt, and refine and further develop their beliefs by bouncing them off other people and listening to the feedback. My hope is not that this book present a list of traits that become universally accepted as a definition of mental health, but rather that it generate thought about the topic and then that the concept be discussed among friends, classmates, teachers, etc., so that each person can begin to develop his or her own concrete model. Chapter Four will present a few ideas of how you can then use this model in your personal and professional life.

Some people who read the first draft of this book asked me why, if I say this model of health doesn't represent any absolute truth but only my beliefs and observations, I present it in such detail as to have 18 specific traits (Chapter Three). It has been my experience, as both a learner and a teacher, that descriptions that are not presented in enough detail generally do not generate as much thought and discussion as do more detailed descriptions. One of the most frequent, and probably valid, criticisms of the literature connected with the humanistic school of psychology is that often ideas are described in such a shallow manner that the writer's thinking is not fully revealed.

In developing a model, I feel I have one advantage over most people. As a trained encounter (sensitivity) group leader, I have spent a great deal of my time over the last five years as a participant in, and a leader of, this type of group. For those not familiar with the encounter-group concept, it will be described in more detail in Chapter Four. Basically, an encounter group is a group of people who get together in order to actualize their potential (go beyond being "normal"). It is through close, personal contacts with these participants, who have as a major goal in their life becoming mentally healthy, that I have developed the model presented in the next chapter.

I am not very original. I have probably stolen every idea I have from someone else! Aside from fellow encounter-group participants and close friends, I have trouble identifying the sources for many of the ideas herein. Having been a college student for eight years, at three universities, I have had many teachers. Unfortunately, most had no influence on me; however, a few influenced and challenged me with some of their ideas. At this time, it is difficult for me to give different teachers credit for their ideas, because they have all sort of blended together. In those years of school, I read more books than I care to think about. Many of my ideas have come from those books, and I would like to give credit to the authors, but I cannot, because the ideas have been so meshed together that original sources are lost. The bibliography at the end of this book includes most of the major written influences on the ideas in this book. Particular credit should be given to philosophers Fredrich Nietzsche and Alan Watts, psychiatrist R. D. Laing, and psychologists Abraham Maslow and William Schutz.

A last note. It is important to remember that this particular model is culture-bound; that is, it works only in a culture like ours, in which people have time to strive toward reaching their fullest potential. This can happen only after basic needs, e.g., food, shelter, and safety, have been met. It is difficult for a hungry person to be concerned with some of the things described in this book, such as reaching out toward other people to form meaningful relationships. They first need to be concerned with getting dinner on the table. These basic needs have been met by the majority, but unfortunately not all, of the people in our culture.

The Model

Chapter Three

The detailed model of the mentally healthy person presented in this chapter should encourage you to develop your own model, one that is correct for you, as this one is correct for me at this time. The basis for my development of this model has been my experiences with persons whom I consider either to be self-actualizing in general or at least to have a number of specific self-actualizing personality traits. The difficulty here is that it is often impossible to accurately communicate experiences through words. When I read the following paragraph by my friend Nietzsche (I say "my friend" because even though he died well before I was born, I have spent so much time communicating with him and his ideas this past year that he seems like a friend), it seemed as if he were speaking directly to me as I was writing this book:

> We no longer esteem ourselves sufficiently when we communicate ourselves. Our true experiences are not at all garrulous. They could not communicate themselves even if they tried. That is because they lack the right word. Whatever we have words for, that we have already got beyond. In all talk there is a grain of contempt. Language, it seems, was invented only for what is average, medium, communicable. With language the speaker immediately vulgarizes himself.
>
> (Kaufmann, 1954, p.530)

To help communicate the meaning of the specific traits I have included in the model of mental health, I have developed two mythical characters, Frank and Allison. Assume that these two people have similar backgrounds—both come from small, middle-class families, both were raised in an urban area, and both are now attending a large, eastern university. Frank is a normal, reasonably happy person. He is *not sick* by any means, but by the definition of this model, he is not mentally healthy, either. If you are not sure what Frank looks like, look around you; Frank is everywhere. Is he in your mirror? Allison, on the other hand, possesses the traits of a mentally healthy person, but to the extreme that she appears (and in fact is) unreal; however the behaviors and attitudes ascribed to Allison are possible and are a composite of behaviors of actual people I have encountered. The thing to keep in mind is that even the healthiest person is not fully developed; there is always room for growth. This is why psychologists talk about the self-actualizing as opposed to the self-actualized person. Although every trait or cluster of traits described in this chapter is possible, I doubt that anyone has reached near his or her full potential in all of these areas.

Before going on to the model, there are a few more things I want to say about Frank and Allison. First, having a healthy female and an average male does not in any way imply that females are healthier than males. Both males and females need to overcome certain sex-bound pressures in order to achieve mental health. One such pressure for males concerns the expression of *all* feelings, e.g., "Men don't cry." One such pressure for females is the notion of passivity. In short, mental health is not the exclusive domain of either sex. But since mental health, as defined here, includes overcoming sex-role stereotyping and limitations, it is the domain of those persons more concerned with being human than with being a good man or woman.

Second, I want to emphasize that Allison is "too good to be true"; she is not real–she's a myth. As such, she is not a standard to aspire to. Indeed, later in this chapter I state my belief that it is a sign of a lack of health to try to live up to the standard of myths. Allison is merely an idea in the same way that Jonathan Livingston Seagull (Bach, 1970) is an idea.

Another way to think of Frank and Allison is that both of them are part of each of us. Every person, not only the most average but even the sickest among us, has some areas of personal existence that do move forward, grow, and develop in a full way. This part of us, this need to grow, is the Allison in us.

Every person, even the healthiest, has times when they want to fit in, be liked, be secure, even if this security requires us to give up part of our unique self. This is the Frank in us.

Mental health, then, can be seen not as an all-or-nothing situation, but rather as dependent on the number and kinds of traits one has fully developed and how important one considers these fully developed traits to be in relation to those traits within us that we see as insufficiently developed. The relative importance of these traits can be determined only by the individual in question. This is why I stated in Chapter Two that no one (no matter how well trained) can really rank anyone else in terms of mental health. An example using the trait of self-concept, which will be discussed later in this chapter, is: Person A and Person B both like almost everything about themselves (high self-esteem) except their physical appearance. Both consider themselves unattractive. Person A spends a great deal of time thinking and feeling unattractive and is therefore shy in dealing with the opposite sex. In fact, Person A's whole life style is affected by this feeling. Person B also feels unattractive but spends very little time thinking about it. It is generally an unimportant facet of life. In terms of the absolute number of traits one feels good or bad about, both Person A and Person B are similar. We cannot, however, assume that both persons have equal self-esteem, because it is obvious here that Person B feels better about his or her self than does Person A. (This issue raises the question of the validity of a scientific approach to the study of people, whereby statistics with little personal meaning are collected as the data to be analyzed. For those interested in a further pursuit of this question of method, see Giorgi, 1970.) It is also a mistake to assume that any one trait can distinguish the healthy person from the average person.

To summarize this issue: Frank and Allison are used only as communication tools to help me suggest the meaning of some of the traits listed in this chapter. For many of the character traits listed in the mental-health model, I will try to briefly describe the related behaviors and attitudes that might be expected from Frank (the average person) and Allison (the healthy person).

In order to be able to understand the traits or behaviors of any one person, it is important to keep in mind that the traits exist only as part of a whole, functioning person. The traits do not stand in isolation. They are interrelated and interdependent. The gestalt (whole person) is more than the sum of the various parts. The whole is the sum of the parts plus the results of the interaction between the parts. To be able to understand Allison or the model, the specific traits need to be considered not only in and of themselves, but also in relation to how you see the total functioning of the mentally healthy person.

In presenting the model, I will first describe the 18 specific character traits that I think are most important in the personality structure of the mentally healthy person. Then, a more general, global definition of mental health will be presented. Hopefully, this will help you tie together these specific and sometimes seemingly unrelated traits into a general theory of mental health. The traits are not listed in any order of importance or logic, except for the first and the last traits; the other 16 could be presented in any order.

1. A Love and Valuing of Life

This trait underlies all of the other traits of the mentally healthy person. It is so basic that it becomes the background through which all else in the person's life emerges. It is a stance toward life, similar to what Viktor Frankl calls the "will to live" (1959) in his explanation of how people lived through prolonged confinement in Nazi concentration camps. It is a valuing of not only one's own life, but all living things as well, including animals and plants. It is also a concern not only for life itself, but also about the quality of existence of all living things.

More than anything else, this trait involves living in what Keen (1972) calls a "human space," an understanding of the world in terms of human experience. As Keen points out, living in the human space is partly living with tragedy; consequently, many of us choose to experience the world through more abstract spaces. For example, if we look at war through a human space, we get in touch with the incredible grief of widowhood, orphanhood, homelessness, and the real possibility of nonbeing for thousands of persons. If we look at war through an abstract political space, we can see the world as being saved from communism or imperialism (depending on which side we are on), and then we can feel proud rather than depressed.

If we look at the world through a scientific space, e.g., medicine, we can justify keeping people alive at all costs. If, however, we consider the nature of such an experience for the patient and his or her family, we might make another decision. However, this is a decision most people find difficult to make; it is much easier to look at this type of situation from a medical rather than a human-space viewpoint. A mentally healthy person, for the most part, understands and experiences the world in terms of human space.

Frank sees only human life as valuable. Ever since he was a youngster, he has gone hunting and fishing with his father. Frank sees the killing of animals as a legitimate sport. Frank lacks the ability to consider what the world is like for other people. He sees his own experience as the basis for all truths and final judgments. As a result, Frank can be very cruel to those persons whom he considers to be different and inferior. For example, he often teases (either directly or behind their back) ugly girls and people who stutter.

Allison seems to have a special place in her heart for living things. Her dormitory room is filled with plants. Ever since she was a young girl, Allison has had pets living with her. She believes that living things can never be owned, for life possesses

itself. For example, when people ask her if a dog is hers, she answers, "No, he does not belong to me; he belongs to himself, but he does live with me."

Although Allison considers herself a political liberal, she is very confused about the question of abortion. She sees too many of her proabortion friends as being somewhat unconcerned about the basic value of life, yet she also sees many antiabortion people as being unconcerned with the issue of quality of life. She is strongly against capital punishment; when wars are fought, she sees everyone as losing. Victory, to her, can never be measured in terms of the number of enemy soldiers killed.

Allison considers all political, social, and personal issues in terms of what it would be like to be involved in the particular situation. She experiences the world in human-space terms. This, by the way, is not something that she makes an extra effort to do; it is her natural, intuitive, day-to-day way of experiencing the world.

2. Physical Health

This concept is very simple; it means considering your body as an important part of you and taking care of it. It does not necessarily mean looking attractive. It certainly does not mean spending a lot of money on the latest fashions or spending a half hour before each social engagement covering up your imperfections and adolescent pimples. It does mean not being very over- or underweight (unless there is a medical reason for it). It does mean eating properly and getting adequate amounts of rest and exercise. It generally means feeling good by being in good physical condition. In short, mental health cannot be separated from physical health, for the two are so interrelated as to be inseparable. Your body is the way you extend yourself in your world. Your body is not something that your mind or soul possesses or puts up with; it is you, and when your body ceases to function, your existence in the world ends.

3. Time Competence

This trait refers to a time orientation which emphasizes the present. The mentally healthy person lives mostly in the here and now (today) and values today for its own sake, not just as a stepping stone toward tomorrow's goals. This does not mean that the past or future are totally ignored. Mentally healthy people are not so pleasure-oriented that they cannot plan for the future; also, they have the ability to learn from their past experiences. It is mostly a question of balance, with the weight on the present. The examples below may help to clarify this point.

In a number of ways, Frank does not use time competently. Even though he dislikes college, he is in college and wants to go to graduate school. In order to get a Ph.D., he is willing to work from eight to ten years at something that does not interest him, because he believes that the way to happiness is through earned status. (This concept of happiness is only a myth, as indicated by the high rates of suicide and physical illness among the highly educated.) Frank is so busy pleasing instructors to get good grades that he hardly ever takes advantage of the many other learning opportunities a college community offers.

This future orientation that Frank displays occurs in epidemic proportions in our culture. One reason for this type of orientation is our educational system, one of the most important socialization influences we ever experience. Schools are run in a way which not only functionally teaches children, but also emphasizes a cultural valuing toward a future orientation. Some of the lessons which children are taught in school on any given day hold no interest and are of no practical use to the pupils. Children are forced to learn such lessons because it "will be important to know some day." Similarly, young people are frequently told to deny themselves certain physical pleasures now because these same pleasures will be more pleasurable later only if the pleasure is forsaken now.

Unfortunately, most of us never outgrow this valuing of the future. Frank really believes that things will change as soon as he gets his final college degree. He doesn't realize that there will *always* be just one more promotion, just one more reason to play along for a little while longer before he will be happy. Frank believes that something that happens today, to be valuable, should have a direct link to future success. Chapter One (the poem) does not reflect Frank's thoughts. According to his value system, it is better to avoid the pains of separation than to develop a relationship with a limited future.

Time competence—focusing on the present—cannot be achieved if one is stuck in the past. Frank has a dull social life; he does not date much. He spends much of his time worrying about his past social failures, and this worry immobilizes his social life in the present. He does not ask girls for dates because he does not want to be rejected by them, as he was in high school.

Allison's time orientation is quite different from Frank's. She went to college for two years and then quit because she had no real goal and did not want to be going only for a degree. After working at a day-care center for a year, she went back to school, wanting to be a teacher. Allison does not get the grades she is capable of attaining, because she spends much of her time learning outside the classroom, e.g., attending lectures and cultural events around the university and doing volunteer work for a local Head Start agency. Allison now enjoys school.

Allison has the ability to form long-lasting relationships, but she also sees temporary ones as having meaning, in that the growing involved in each relationship remains a permanent part of her. She could have written Chapter One.

4. Internal Locus of Validation and Motivation

Our culture teaches us to validate (evaluate) ourselves mostly through feedback we receive from others. We learn to feel okay about ourselves only when our parents say we did well on a given task or when our teacher gives us a gold star, or when the college instructor gives us an A. Consequently, our main motivational force in life seems to be to please others, to do what others want and expect us to do in the way they want and expect us to do it.

The mentally healthy person is able to transcend this cultural teaching and learns to evaluate his or her own behavior and performance. Products have meaning for the mentally healthy person insofar as they serve the individual's purpose.

If the mentally healthy person feels that he or she has done a task as well as possible, he or she will feel good about it. This good feeling would prevail even if the work was negatively evaluated by others. The primary questions become: "How do I feel about what I have done?" and "Can I own (take responsibility for) my behavior?"

There are two factors which make this a difficult trait to explain. First, if the mentally healthy person transcends (goes beyond) what he or she has learned and begins a process of self-evaluation, how does the person do this ? I don't know the answer to that. I am sure that some people are more self-evaluative (as opposed to outside-evaluative) than most others, and one day I hope to discover how they got that way. If one of you has found the answer, perhaps you will write to me and share some of your ideas.

Second, the role of feedback from others is a somewhat complicated matter. Certainly, a mentally healthy person listens to and even values feedback from other persons. One of the important differences between Frank and Allison has to do with the way each of them internalizes and uses feedback. A healthy person considers feedback from another person as one other opinion, to be used in conjunction with other opinions and with self-evaluation to help arrive at desired conclusions or to make decisions. Too often, most of us consider the evaluation of others, particularly authority figures, as some sort of absolute judgment about us.

Frank, like most of us, has joined the rat race. The primary motivation for most of his behavior is to get people to judge him the winner in what he sees as a competitive world. He feels that he is better than his fellow students when he gets an A from a teacher, and he feels inferior to them when they get a higher grade than he does. Grades are emphasized over learning, so that he always chooses "easy" teachers over harder, and possibly better, ones.

Allison, by contrast, goes to school to learn. Like Frank, she likes to get good grades. She understands that high grades are sometimes helpful (in terms of jobs or graduate school). However, she doesn't take the grades so seriously that her self-esteem is dependent on them. She understands that a grade is only one person's evaluation of her work in one class and that sometimes it is a valid evaluation and sometimes not. She spends most of her time working on her carefully considered goals, both professional and social, rather than working strictly for a grade. She sees progress in a classroom as progress toward knowledge, not progress toward an A.

Socially, she acts the same way to external evaluation. She does the things that make her feel good about herself, not those things her peers pressure her into doing. She does not always follow the socially accepted norm. Allison does not use drugs, as many of her friends do, nor does she attend church, as her parents do. Neither taking drugs nor attending church feels right for her. Her attitude is summed up by the quote on a poster she has in her room: "In a rat race everyone loses, 'cause even if you win the race, you're still just a rat!"

I want to add a personal note here about this trait, because I think it may be helpful to some of you reading this. A few years ago I was in a short-term therapy group. At the time, I was considering quitting school, even though I had only a half year of classes left, because I disliked it so much. As I was trying to work through this issue in the group, the leader said something that I will probably never forget. He said that I often spent time doing something I didn't want to do without even knowing why I was doing it. (I was even doing this in the therapy group, another example of how therapy usually mirrors daily issues in what some people falsely call the unreal environment of therapy.) He suggested that every time I found myself doing something I did not really want to be doing, I ask myself what the payoff is for doing this. If the payoff seems worth it, e.g., getting a college degree, then stick with it. No one lives a life that can be arranged so that the person does what he or she wants all the time. However, if the payoff for doing what you do not want to do is unclear (for example, something you do because you have always done it that way before) or is not worth it, then stop doing it and see what happens.

I pass this advice on because it has been very helpful to me in making day-to-day, and sometimes long-term, decisions about my life. Hopefully, some of you may also find this way of thinking useful.

5. High Risk-taking Behavior

From infancy to old age, we grow the most when we take some personal risks. By this I mean that we learn the most about ourselves and how to cope with our environment when we do things that are different from our habitual behavior. When we do things differently, it is a risk because we do not know what outcome to expect, and the possibility exists that the outcome will not be a pleasant one. Children learn and grow more than adults do, not just because there is more for them to learn, but also because they are not afraid to fail. None of us would be able to walk now if, when we were learning how, we had been afraid of falling down. Some time during childhood, the average person learns to equate mistakes with failures. So then mistakes, rather than being part of the learning process, become a judgment about us—we are failures.

For adults, the process is more complex. We try to avoid feeling badly about ourselves for there seems to be a cultural value on being content. Depression is something you try to talk a friend out of rather than let him or her experience the entire range of feelings and learn from them. To avoid feeling badly about ourselves, we learn not to do risky things. When Frank wants to meet someone he thinks he would like as a friend, he makes small overtures toward that person. He never really extends himself until he gets very clear signs of "I like you, too" from the person. Since most other people are like Frank in this respect—average—many possible relationships never connect for want of someone to make the first clear move.

Allison knows that rejection hurts, that it makes her feel badly about herself. She also knows that meaningful relationships are important for her growth, and she doesn't want all the missed connections that she sees the Franks of the world experiencing. Therefore, she risks rejection and clearly extends herself to others. She knows that it is those things that scare her the most that she most needs to do. She joined her first sensitivity group primarily because she was so scared at the prospect that she needed to find out what it was about them that scared her.

6. Synergy

The next two traits are very closely related. The difference is that when I talk of synergy, I am referring to ideas, concepts, or things external to the person, whereas the next trait (accepts contradictions in self) refers to concepts internal to the person, such as certain feelings about oneself. The concept of synergy was first articulated by anthropologist Ruth Benedict, and my definition is derived from her studies in anthropology. For a more detailed description of the original definition, see Maslow (1971, Chapter 14).

The lived world of people is a very complicated and ambiguous place; it can be no other way, because people are the essence of contradictions and ambiguity. Many people avoid the anxiety of living in an uncertain world by structuring their world into a series of dichotomies. Life then consists of black or white, good or bad, right or wrong, liberal or conservative, democracy or communism, etc. Perception of events is thus distorted, so that events fit into predetermined categories. Persons high in synergy represent a transcending of the dichotomization of the world. They not only see the gray between the black and white, but also recognize that the meaning given to black and white itself is always shifting and dependent on person, place, and time.

When Allison considers social issues, she has the ability to look at the many facets of any given issue and see that usually, many possible viewpoints or interpretations contain elements of truth. This does not mean that she is always a "middle-of-the-roader," never making a commitment to an issue or taking a stand. Rather, when she does take a stand, she understands that those taking different positions usually also have some valid reasons for their position. When Frank takes a position on a social issue, however, he does so with complete confidence that God is on his side and that other viewpoints are taken only by ignorant or immoral (or both) people.

This is one issue on which many people have opposite viewpoints. Maslow, for example, believes that there is a basic definition of "rightness" and "wrongness"; this definition is not culturally relative, but rather, is shared by all self-actualizing people, regardless of their cultural background. Here, as with every other trait, you need to decide which idea is right for you, since we professionals often disagree among ourselves.

7. Accepts Contradictions in Self

Just as the synergistic person rejects polarities in issues (not seeing them as having an absolute "rightness" and "wrongness"), the mentally healthy person rejects polarities within his or her self-image. Since *part of our humanness includes having parts of every possible human trait within us*, the mentally healthy person does not see himself or herself as being one thing and therefore not another. Since many of our traits seem to be at odds with one another, great confusion can occur. The great majority of people deal with this confusion by denying parts of themselves, accepting only those traits which seem in harmony

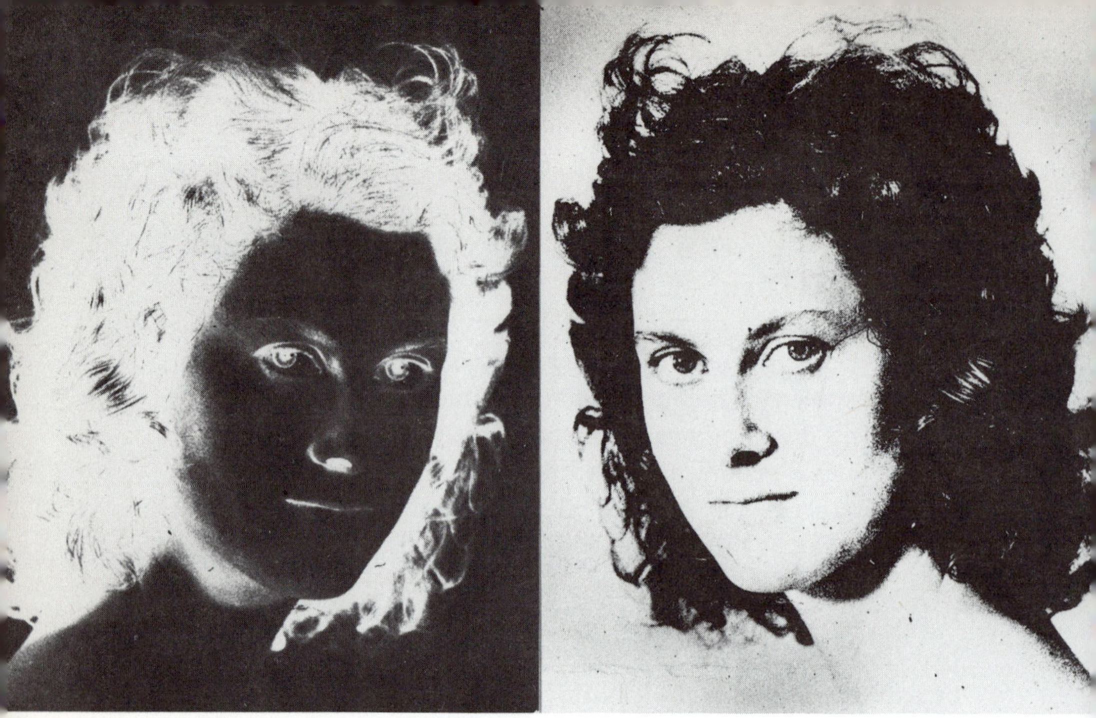

with one another. Our culture seems to value this harmony in people because it makes them somewhat predictable. Mentally healthy people deal with the possible confusion by having a true emotional acceptance—a total acceptance, not just a realization—of all parts of themselves, even those that seem to be contradictory.

A story told by Dr. Sol Rosenberg, a respected psychologist, may help to illustrate this concept. Dr. Rosenberg was in a brief demonstration-type therapy group led by Dr. Frederick (Fritz) Perls, the well-known gestalt therapist. At the end of the session, Fritz asked the participants if there was anything they wanted to clear up with him. Sol said that there was one thing he didn't like about Fritz, namely, every time Fritz did something good in the group, he looked to the audience (remember, this was a demonstration group with an audience) for approval and recognition. In response, Fritz asked Sol what he felt he (Sol) did particularly well. Sol thought for a minute and then said, "Well, I am a better than average tennis player." Fritz asked Sol to get up and stroll around the room the way a better than average tennis player would do it. Sol thought that this would be an easy task; after all, he had already shared much of himself with the group. He got up, but his legs froze; he could not move. No interpretation by Fritz was necessary. Sol realized that he had rejected the show-off part of himself as being "bad" (the "nice people are humble" myth) and that what he had really objected to was not Fritz's show-offness, but *his own*, which he tried to hide. Once he came to this realization, Sol was able to reincorporate this rejected part of himself into his total being. Now, he is able to be different things at different times. When it feels right for him to show off, he can do it; when it feels right to be humble, he can do that, too. This is an excellent example of someone reowning a formerly disowned part of himself.

Frank has learned that people respond better to him when he behaves in a predictable, consistent manner. This is especially true when his behaviors are those which most people would label "good." Because of this, Frank has rejected parts of himself. For example, he has rejected the concept of his dependency; he sees himself as a totally independent person (à la John Wayne). Frank is humble, never a show-off; is a nice person, never a bastard; is happy, almost never acts sad (a plastic smile); and is always liking, never expressing hate.

Allison is aware that her inconsistent behaviors keep some people away from her. She is willing to pay this price for her growth. Allison knows that at times she is independent and able to act on her own, but she is also aware of her dependency on others to meet many of her needs. Most times, she is a nice person; but there are times when she feels like a bitch and is able to act her feelings. She is generally a happy person, but she also experiences and expresses sadness. She values this because she knows that it is her sadness which makes her happiness meaningful. Allison generally likes people and often establishes love relationships. She is aware that all her relationships contain a few elements of dislike and hate (we all have a hatred, as well as a love, for our parents), and she is able to deal with this ambivalence. One of Allison's favorite sayings is: "Consistency is the hobgoblin of small minds."

8. Ability for Authentic Communication

The first step toward developing this trait is awareness. Before anyone can communicate something to someone else, one must first be aware of what's happening; one must be aware of all the thoughts and feelings inside oneself.

After awareness comes the willingness to express what's happening inside of you—your thoughts and your feelings—to other people. Most people are not willing to risk sharing themselves in that way. It is much easier for most of us to talk about "safe" things—objects, other people, or oneself in the past or future tense. The scary thing is expressing what is happening to us in the present, right now. Authentic communication means expressing what you are feeling with your entire body, not just through words. There is something less than authentic about saying to someone, "I am angry with you," while smiling. Our face can show the anger, too.

The mentally healthy person who is open with his or her communication knows almost instinctively when it is appropriate to be open and when openness is dysfunctional. For example, it is not necessarily healthy to cry at work every time you feel sad—among other things, you may get fired. But it is surprising to me how many men do not cry in front of their friends or even their wives. When this happens (or doesn't happen), it is their image of what a strong man is that is controlling them; they are not controlling their image. The mentally healthy person can control his or her emotions, but this *control includes an expression of emotions as often as possible.*

Authentic communication is effective communication. It gets across to other people what is happening to you and what your needs are. Other people can then help you meet your needs, as you can for them. For example, if you have a need to be hugged by your spouse, lover, friend, or parent, there are three ways to cope with this need for physical contact. The most authentic and effective way is to clearly make your need(s) known to other(s). Usually, a simple "Hey, I need to be hugged" gets the job done. Of course, the risk is in dealing with the unpleasant feelings the few times this direct approach doesn't work. The other options decrease, in one case eliminate, the possibility of satisfying your needs. One of these ways is to try to manipulate the other person(s) into meeting your needs. An example of such manipulation is for person A to pout and stare sadly at the floor every time he or she does not get his or her own way, so as to get person B to feel bad about the situation and give in to person A. But this works only some of the time, depending on how good a manipulator one is; in no cases have I seen it work as often as a direct expression of feeling. Often, bad feelings will erupt within a relationship when one's needs are not met after a half-hearted attempt to express a particular need or desire. That is like saying "It's your fault you didn't understand my half-message" or "You didn't read my mind and meet my needs." The third possible option is to tell yourself that your needs aren't important or that you "shouldn't" have them and then forget about trying to meet them. This option is related to trait 7, not accepting parts, needs, of yourself.

Effective communication lets everyone in a relationship know what is happening in that relationship. This can help determine when changes in direction are needed and how to make those desired changes. It is not surprising that many marriage counselors work exclusively on a couple's communication, believing that once the two partners develop effective communication skills, they will often be able to solve their own problems. In short, since I believe that most of our growth takes place in interpersonal relationships, authentic, effective communication is vitally important in growing toward mental health.

The following example of Frank is typical of many of us, given the child-rearing practices and attitudes in our culture. The first people Frank (as is true for all children) got angry at were his parents. A major function of Frank's parents was to socialize him, e.g., toilet training. This meant that they required Frank to do things he did not want to do. When Frank displayed his anger toward his parents, they hit him, punished him, or withdrew their love from him. (Many parents have trouble dealing with anger or aggression directed toward them by their children. Parents permit their children to hit the Bo Bo doll, but not mother. It is O.K. to say "I hate you" to your friend next door, but not to your father.) Frank soon learned not to display the anger he was feeling. To this day, Frank has trouble expressing anger. He feels it is unsafe to get angry, for if he does, others will only withdraw their friendship (love) from him. Consequently, he keeps things inside. Frank will probably get an ulcer or have periodic explosions, blowing a few small things way out of proportion.

Anger seems to be the one emotion that people have the greatest trouble dealing with and expressing. The following theory of anger has been helpful to me in learning to deal with my own anger. It is a part of a larger theory of personality called transactional analysis, whose major spokeman has been Dr. Eric Berne. According to this view, when someone does something that makes you angry, it is as though that person was giving you some trading stamps. Trading stamps are just like those you get in the supermarket; you paste them in a book (your head) and eventually cash them in for a prize. The more stamps you collect, the bigger the prize you can demand. The most expensive prizes in the catalog are murder and suicide, but only a small percentage of people save for these big prizes. Most people choose smaller items; among the more popular are physical problems (tension headaches, ulcers, stomach trouble, etc.), temper explosions, and even depression. (In working with depressed persons in therapy situations, clinicians have often found that behind the mask of depression is a great deal of unexpressed anger, which often is not even recognized as such by the person. In a sense, depression is anger turned inward.) Anger seems to have physical properties which do not just go away if you ignore them. Therefore, according to this theory, the best way to spend your anger stamps is in small numbers, as soon as you can. If someone does something that gets you angry, spend the stamps by yelling back or doing whatever makes you feel good, short of physical harm. If you choose not to spend any anger stamps on that person (because that person is your boss or teacher, for example), find another way to spend the stamps, e.g., pound on a sofa or snap at a friend for a few seconds (that's what friends are for). Remember, the more stamps you spend, the lighter the load you carry around.

Frank also has difficulty expressing positive emotions. He doesn't usually take the risk (trait 5) of telling someone "I really felt good being with you last night" or "I love you." It has been my experience that whenever people say that they will be honest with one another (e.g., in a sensitivity group), they always fear that a great deal of negativism will flow out and that someone will get hurt. Usually, however, I've found that there is much more that is positive and unsaid, e.g., "I want to be your friend," than there is negative.

Allison not only can express her anger (and love) to others, she also welcomes it when others express their feelings to her. She knows that there are things about her that sometimes makes people angry. Until Allison feels that anger can be expressed freely without having it destroy the relationship, she cannot trust the friendship.

9. Takes Responsibility for Oneself and for One's Life

Although it may seem trivial to examine the language a person uses, it can be extremely important in terms of getting a total picture of a person. Below are some examples of things Frank would say. Listen to the people around you. Do you hear similar things? Do you say the same kinds of things?

> "I can't go to the football game because I have to visit my mother."
>
> "I should not have sex with you before we are married."
>
> "I can't express my anger directly toward him."

Words like "can't," "have to," and "should" are examples of not taking responsibility (in our mind and our language) for our own behavior. Instead, we give control to some outside, mysterious force. Think about it. There are very few things you *can't* do; there is almost nothing you *have* to do, and "should" is such an ambiguous word that it means nothing when used in communication. Yet the average person often uses these words every day.

Allison was in an encounter group and made the following statement to another member. "I can't get angry at you, because my mother never let me express anger." The group leader asked her to look around the room and point to her mother. At first, she was puzzled, but suddenly Allison had an insight as to the meaning of the leader's statement. Since her mother was not present, she could not be used as an excuse, and Allison was forced to own up to her behaviors. She then had the choice of either expressing her anger and seeing what the consequences would be, or saying, "I'm not ready to take that risk, so I choose not to do it." Allison might express the same ideas as Frank did, but in the following manner:

> "I choose to give up the football game so that I may visit my mother."
>
> "I will not have sex with you before marriage because it does not feel right to me."
>
> "I am afraid to express my anger directly to him."

Another common way many people avoid taking responsibility for their behavior is through the use of the third person when they are really talking about themselves. Vague, third-person pronouns, such as "people" or "they," take the place of "I" when the speaker is not ready to risk revealing any of his or her self.

> Frank (speaking to a group of friends):
>
> "People in our culture often have sexual hang-ups because of the way we are raised." (He is trying to get some helpful information from his friends.)
>
> Allison (also speaking to friends):
>
> "This is difficult for me to speak about, but I am having some conflicts concerning sex, and I think that mabe you can help me by giving me some feedback about myself."

The idea of taking responsibility for oneself is related to the idea of free will. If you were not free to make choices about your life, no one could expect you to be responsible for your life. Thus, I think that the debate in psychology and philosophy of free will versus determinism is an example of people dichotomizing their world. No person is totally free, yet no person is totally predetermined by past experience.

People and the world coinhabit each other. Neither people nor the world "caused" the other, yet neither can exist without the other. People exist in a world, not in isolation. The world is given meaning by people. Each influences the other, which in turn has an influence. In this way, people can be seen as both active (in that they influence their world) and passive (in that they are influenced by their world).

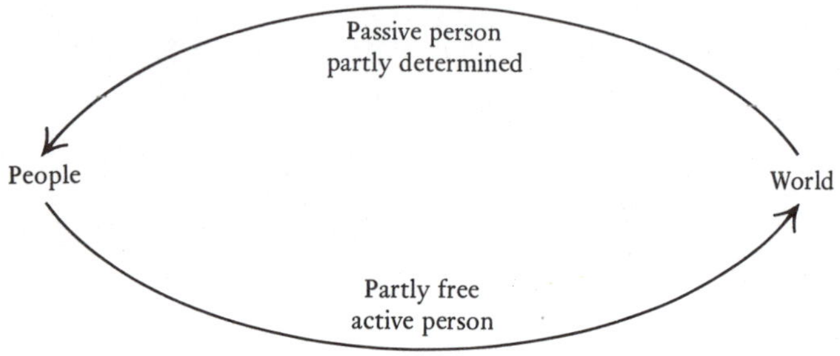

Because of this, people can be said to have *situational freedom.* The world creates a situation for them to respond to, but the choice of responses is still up to each person. In fact, a person is so free that he or she can make any response to any situation within physical limitations, except the response of not responding. People must choose—there is no way not to— but that is the only limitation (except those limitations that are bodily).

For example, your lived world right now consists in part of this book. The context (situation) in which the book exists may be that a teacher required you to read it and is planning to give you a test on this material. That is the situation you respond to; however, it is still up to you to decide how to respond. Under no conditions do you *have* to read this book. Presently, you are choosing to read it. Suppose the teacher gave an exam and no one chose to show up to take it?

10. Ability to Give and Receive Love

This trait is so interrelated with trait 12 (a healthy concept of "self") that I do not want to spend much time discussing it now. However, it is important enough to mention separately. The ability to give and to receive love—this capacity for intimate contact—requires two things. First, it requires a high degree of self-esteem (trait 12). I have seen posters which say: "The most important word is "we"; the least important word is "I." Personally, I cannot understand this. I think that my marriage is a healthy, loving "we," but it is that way only because it consists of two, growing "I's." When the "I's" neglect themselves, the "we" will soon deteriorate.

> "I am in love with me
> For without me
> How could I have experienced
> All the love of you?"
>
> Torbett (1968, p.58)

The second necessary factor is the ability and willingness to trust. To Erik Erikson, this is the basis of all human development. To trust is to take a risk. If you trust someone and he or she lets you down, you may be hurt and experience pain. If you trust your own judgments that attract you to someone and the relationship turns out to be a negative experience, you are not likely to feel good about your judgments. However, not to trust is also to take a risk. You risk losing potentially meaningful relationships. I see the healthy person as one who takes the risk of trusting—one who does not spend a lot of time and energy putting up protective shields.

11. The Ability to See Through Cultural Symbols and Myths

The ability to separate symbols and myths from the "facts" they supposedly represent is one of the most important traits a

mentally healthy person can have. It is also the most difficult trait to explain, since an impersonal communicator (a writer) is limited to the use of symbols (words) for the communication.

We developed symbols to help us communicate concepts (ideas) and feelings to others. Over the years, we have become so good at the use of these symbols that in many cases the symbols have replaced the concept they were intended to communicate. The following example is so far-fetched that many of you may laugh and think, "I'm not that stupid to ever let it happen to me." If this is the case, think again. I am suggesting that this happens to you every day and that often, you do not even realize it.

> In the eighteenth century, England changed its calendar from December 2nd to December 14th in order to be more consistent with the calendars of surrounding countries. When the change was announced, there was a riot because many people thought the government was taking 13 days out of their lives.

Every day, many people react to symbols in the same way that the English reacted to the calendar change. For example, school grades were meant to symbolize the teacher's evaluation of what a student had learned. Today, however, many people equate grades with knowledge itself. To many students (and parents and teachers), the goal of getting a B average is the same as the goal of learning. Universities guard transcripts in fireproof vaults, but leave library books on open shelves. Young people have been sent to jail for burning a cloth symbol (the flag), and respect for authority is often judged by clothing. A quote which has meaning for me (the source is unremembered) is:

> "A wedding ring can never symbolize our love because no one else can ever touch what we have."

A myth is defined here as a statement presented as representing the human condition, but which in reality presents cultural untruths which can be either explicitly stated or implicitly passed on. Many people experience a great deal of discomfort when they compare themselves to these myths, and of course they always come out second best. A mentally healthy person can see that the myths are untrue (that there is a discrepancy between these myths and the facts of life) and will not try to live up to these unrealistic expectations. Myths can be presented in the form of idealized persons (John Wayne or a beautiful model) or in the form of ideas that get passed along. What we see of such myths is not their existence in the every-day lived world that we experience, but rather the result of much expense, make-up, rehearsals, scripts, and retakes. This fact sometimes gets lost, and many women feel badly about themselves because they do not look like a model. Many men feel badly and try to hide the fact that they aren't quite "the man" that John Wayne is. The point is, John Wayne isn't "that man" either, and the person who can see through the myth knows this.

Sex is one area in which ideas–myths–are passed along. For example, almost every study in this area shows that practically all men and the majority of women masturbate and that it is a very healthful form of sexuality, particularly (but not exclusively) for adolescents. Somehow, the myth still persists, and gets passed along, that this type of behavior is unhealthful or something to be ashamed of; therefore, it is almost never talked about. Even worse, many people feel guilty about engaging in this healthful behavior. Probably every college counseling center in the country sees a number of students each year who are dealing with this guilt.

Another area of cultural myth concerns the role of women in our society. I see the women's movement, which is becoming increasingly popular in this country, as an important tool in helping women to both see through the myths of what a woman "should be" and become aware of their full potential.

12. A Healthy Concept of "Self"

A healthy self-concept has a number of components. Although the five components are presented here as separate aspects, please remember that they are all integrated and are not really separable.

A. Acceptance of a Nondistorted Image of Self

Experiments have shown that when our environment gives us unpleasant information about ourselves, we can (without knowing it) protect ourselves by not perceiving the information or by distorting it so that it appears less threatening. This distortion or lack of perception is commonly known as a defense mechanism. Mentally healthy persons can receive all feedback about themselves so that their picture of themselves is relatively nondistorted. They see themselves as others see them. Mentally healthy persons also generally like what they see. They have a high degree of self-acceptance. This does not mean that they see themselves as being perfect. On the contrary, healthy persons know that there is always room for growth. It means that today they like themselves for today and hope that tomorrow they will be even more like they want to be.

The research evidence in psychology is overwhelming that in order to accept others, we must first be able to accept ourselves. This is why I mentioned in the discussion of trait 10—the ability to give and receive love—that high self-acceptance is important. Without it, a person will find it difficult, and maybe even impossible, to enter into a meaningful relationship with others.

B. Awareness and Acceptance of all Parts of Self

I like to think of the self as having three interrelated and interdependent parts: the emotions of the self, the thoughts of the self, and the physical body of the self. All three parts of the self have components that the culture labels as either good and desirable or bad and undesirable. Many people protect their self-image by a lack of awareness that some so-called undesirable traits are part of them. Other people, aware of their undesirable traits, do not like them and have trouble accepting them. Mentally healthy persons are aware of all aspects of their self. They are also able to accept all aspects of themselves because they understand that everyone possesses part of every trait and that no trait is either good or bad; rather, all traits are part of being human. (This is similar to trait 7—accepting contradictions in self.)

There are a number of emotions which are considered to be undesirable. Previously, I discussed anger and some problems associated with it. Aggression is another emotional area that many of us cannot accept in ourselves. I believe that this is one of the reasons why football is such a popular spectator sport. By identifying with the aggressiveness in someone else, many of us vicariously express our own forbidden feelings.

An area many of us cannot accept in our thought processes is fantasy. Some people accept night dreams because they mistakenly think that they have no control over dreams. However, few people accept, much less admit, having daydreams, because such fantasies often relate to our sexual or power needs.

Experimental studies of the effects of dream deprivation show that when dreams do not take place, behaviors that resemble mental illness occur. Fantasies are not only healthful, but they can also be a source of enjoyment if one allows oneself to relax and get into the experience. Daydreams can also help open new areas of communication if you share with others fantasies you have about them.

Perhaps no part of the self has more blocks to mental growth and health associated with it than the physical body. Most people in our Western culture, if asked the location of their self, would point to their head. It is as if we reject the rest

of our body as being part of our self; rather, the body is treated as a possession of the self. Listen to the language people around you use. Often, you will hear, "I *have* two legs," but rarely do you hear, "I *am* two legs." But, of course, we *are* our body; if not, what are we?

This alienation from our body causes two problems. First, we learn to listen to only part of our body—the cortex (mind)—even though the rest of our body gives us information about ourselves that is valuable and sometimes more accurate than that the mind gives us. I have only recently begun to listen to my body. I have learned that when my chest gets heavy, it usually means that my "self" wants to leave wherever I am at the time. If my leg muscles tighten up as I approach someone, I know that I either do not want to go to that person or that I am afraid to go any closer. I can use this information to help me make decisions about what I want or need to do. The mentally healthy person uses all possible information to make decisions.

Second, alienation from our body is one of the prime causes of sexual conflict, something that occurs in epidemic proportions in our culture. A person who is in touch with his or her self understands (not just with the mind, but with the total self) that something that feels so right, such as an honest sexual relationship, cannot be wrong in as many circumstances as our culture's moral code suggests.

C. Some Insight into Self

Often, I have heard people say, "I know myself completely." I am then sure that the person speaking is either a fool or a liar. We have too many protective mechanisms, such as distortion of threatening information, that keep us from ever completely knowing ourselves. Alan Watts once said that one's conceit of self-knowledge is probably the greatest deceit of all; however, the mentally healthy person does strive to get as much self-knowledge as possible and as a result has more insight into his or her self than most people do.

Allison is continually checking out her behaviors to get the answers to such questions as: "What mechanisms do I use to protect myself when I am afraid of getting hurt in a relationship?" "What does it mean when my hand shakes?" These questions are of no concern to Frank; he is either sure that he knows all there is to know about himself, or he doesn't care.

D. Can be Alone with Self

Although the mentally healthy person highly values relationships with other people, he or she also has the ability and the desire to be alone at times. Alone means not only without other people, but also without the television, radio, etc. These are mechanical escapes from the self.

This concept of aloneness is very different from the socially accepted concept of privacy. Many people use privacy as a way of hiding what they are ashamed of. For example, people hide behind the concept of privacy when they do not tell their friends about their marital difficulties. Aloneness, however, is a positive behavior, a moving toward oneself rather then a moving away from others. An individual shuns social interaction in order to get more in touch with his or her self.

E. Sees Self as Part of a Total Environment

The mentally healthy person understands that selfhood is only part of a total environment, that in isolation one has no meaning. Mentally healthy people have a very real identification with humanity; a part of themselves suffers with every suffering human around the world, and a part of themselves rejoices when others have a reason to rejoice. Because of this understanding that one is part of a total environment, social and ecological issues become important to mentally healthy people, and their behavior includes concern for and involvement in some of these issues.

13. Openness

This trait is different from trait 8, which has to do with an openness in communication with others. Trait 13 is more of an internal openness, an openness within oneself to new information and new values. It includes the ability to learn from others and to learn from oneself, even when that learning may contradict information or positions previously learned. It includes the continual reassessing of what we know and how we feel. The mentally healthy person does not value consistency for its own sake.

Frank is keenly aware of the pressure many people his age feel—to grow up, to be mature. This is certainly a legitimate request by our society. At some time we all need to learn to take more responsibility than was required in our childhood and ado-

lescence. The problem, however, is that a definition of maturation often includes a concern for consistency: "Pick a trade that you will work at for your lifetime"; "Hear all the facts concerning this idea and then form an opinion and stick to it." By reacting to this pressure, Frank becomes very nonflexible (rigid).

In a very real sense, Allison not only values her being (today), but also cherishes her becoming (tomorrow). This becoming is not limited by a preset direction arrived at earlier in life, but instead includes all the wonderful but confusing possibilities that one's existence is.

14. Striving for Congruence Between Values and Life Style

In my opinion, the basic cause of conflict within a person is the discrepancy between one's values and one's way of life, or life style. Mentally healthy people strive for congruence between their values and the way they live. They also have the ability to deal with the conflict or anxiety that does exist; they do not get overwhelmed by it. (I know of no one who lives totally according to his or her beliefs. Even the most courageous among us live out only a portion of their beliefs.)

Frank occasionally gets overwhelmed by this type of anxiety. He prevents it from occurring too often by putting his life style and values closer together. The problem is that the way Frank does this is dysfunctional to his growth as a person. He changes his perceptions and values by making them coincide with his present life patterns, for the sole purpose of reducing stress. Frank is not always aware that he does this. The end result is that he gets a great deal of inaccurate information about his environment. (This is similar to the distortion of perception discussed in trait 12. In psychology, this phenomenon is known as cognitive dissonance, and research has shown that it occurs quite frequently. A more detailed description of this phenomenon can be found in almost any social psychology textbook.

Allison deals with this value/life style conflict in one of two ways, both of which stimulate growth. Often, she takes some risks and engages in new behaviors that are closer to her values than were previous behaviors. The risk is that she never knows the results of the new behaviors before she tries them. When Allison is not ready to risk behavior changes, she has the ability to accept the lack of congruence between her beliefs and her life style. She understands that this is part of the human condition and therefore does not get overwhelmed because of it. Her feeling is that she accepts the difference today and will wait to see what tomorrow brings. But essentially, she tries to follow a saying she once saw on a poster: "Put your life where your mouth is."

15. Problem-solving Ability

Since life is a continuing process of searching for answers to everyday problems (decision-making), the mentally healthy person has the ability to solve problems and to make decisions. Most important, these people have confidence in their problem-solving and decision-making abilities. They understand that they have the capacity to actively control their environment. Allison has a poster which reads: "If you give me a fish, I can eat today; if you teach me to fish, I can eat every day."

16. Appreciation of Everyday Experiences

Mentally healthy people experience beauty every day. They see the uniqueness of each person and of each flower. The moon means something different each night. The oceans, the mountains, and the farmland are all understood to be miracles. Then, of course, there is the beauty of holding hands. A mentally healthy person appreciates art and beauty, but knows that one does not find it only in a museum.

A special form of this appreciation of everyday experience is an appreciation of the human condition, an understanding

that part of all life is suffering unhappiness and unfair situations. A mentally healthy person may be deeply involved in the struggle to improve these conditions, but also has the ability to occasionally laugh at his or her plight. A mentally healthy woman involved in the woman's movement will still be able to laugh at a good male chauvinist joke, just as Dick Gregory—as deeply committed as he is to the black movement—can still laugh and joke about black-white differences.

17. Transcendence

To a person who has never experienced transcendence, the term may represent something so mystical as to lack credibility. The idea of transcendence is, however, important. In Maslow's theory of self-actualization, this concept is separated from all other actualizing traits. To Maslow, there are two types of healthy people—those who can and those who cannot transcend. I would encourage you to read Maslow (1971, Chapters 21 and 22) for a very fine, detailed description of all the various meanings of this concept.

Transcendence means losing oneself (self-consciousness) and briefly identifying with a larger order (going beyond oneself). This identification can be with people, things, or the whole cosmos. It can be the oneness with the world that many Eastern religions see as the highest goal of humans. This identification with something beyond oneself does not mean "I have had similar experiences and so I know how you feel" but rather "I am you and you are me."

Allison spent a weekend camping out with some very close friends. Late on the last evening, after many hours of warm, intimate contact, they were all sitting close together around a campfire, and one person was playing soft music on a guitar. Then something strange happened to Allison. For a period of time (she has no idea how long) she lost touch with herself and instead was one with the circle of other people, the music, the campfire, and even the starry night. Rather than being a person holding hands with the people on either side of her, with others looking at her and she wondering what they were thinking, she was, not the other people per se, but the unity, the circle with its gentle swaying to the music and its oneness with nature. When this experience ended, Allison couldn't really explain it to her friends, or even to herself. She intuitively understood that this peak experience was something she wanted to experience again.

Transcendence can also have more specific meanings. It can mean going beyond certain self-imposed limitations. For example, people can transcend time and not only exist fully in the present, but also have very meaningful links to their historical roots and to future generations. It can mean transcending one's specific culture and country and instead developing an identification with a universe of human species.

Most people, however, would not include transcendence in their own model of mental health. Our culture teaches a valuing of a certain type of experience, those involving a level of consciousness called rationality. This level of reality is presented as not only more valued, but even more real, than other levels of reality. But this is absurd. For example, when you are dreaming, the kind of consciousness or reality you are experiencing is different from that you experience when you are awake. During the dream, the dream material is your existential reality, and the room you are in is the unreal (unexperienced) phenomenon. In fact, not one of you reading this can prove that you are not dreaming now. There is no way for you to know. Any moment, you may wake up in your bed. Perhaps it is this temporary experiencing of a different reality that offers one of the positive possibilities of drug use. However, it is this very aspect, in addition of more legitimate reasons, that scares most people about drug use.

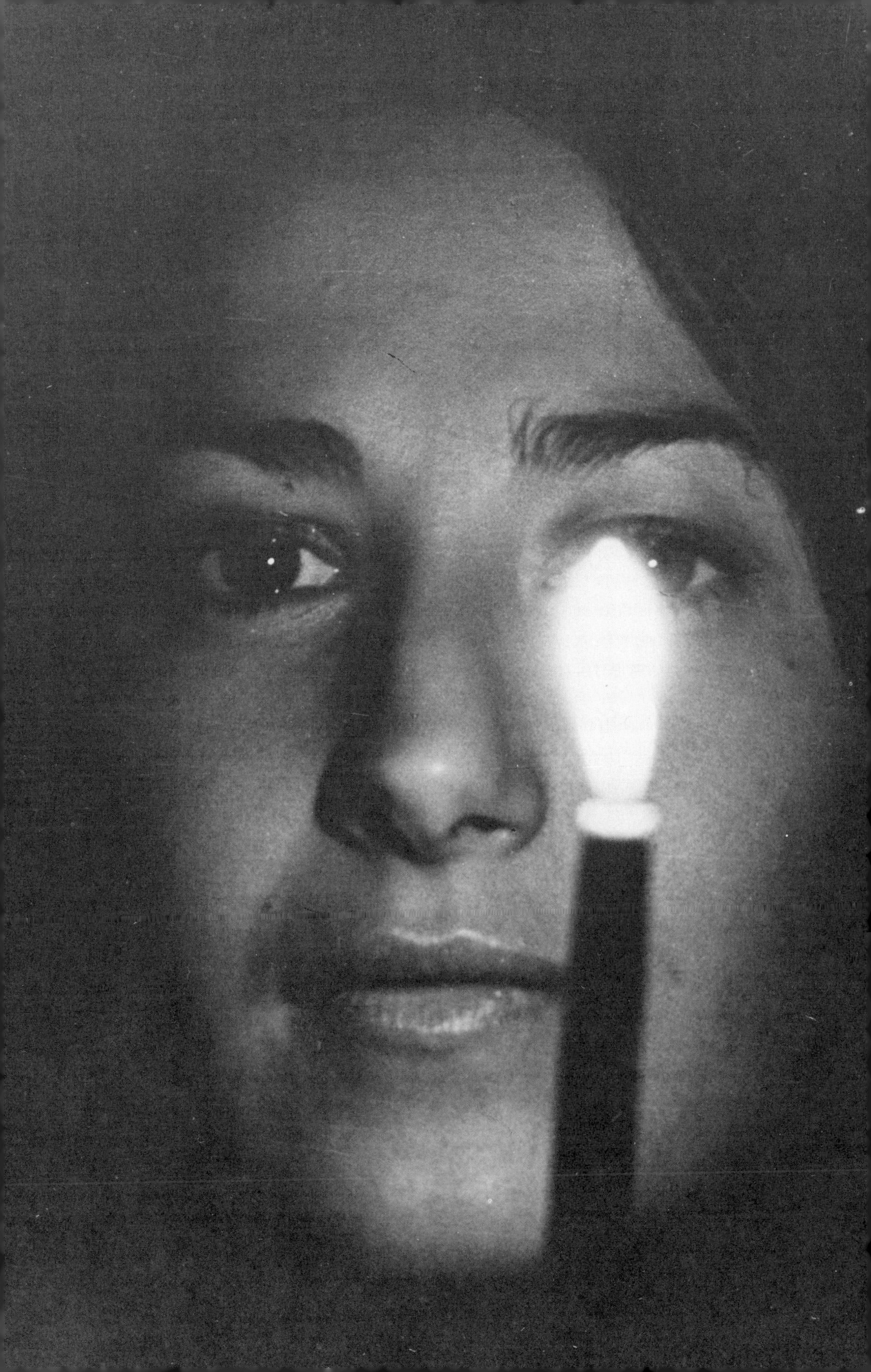

Transcendence, in its best form, just happens to you. It is not induced through meditation or the use of drugs. But you need to be receptive to the experience, because defending yourself from it is easy. Frank (or in this case the Frank inside me) was reading *Knots* by R. D. Laing. After reading about 15 pages, he began to experience strange feelings, as if he were losing himself. Rather than flowing with the experience, he successfully fought it. After a few moments, this strange feeling changed into a familiar one—anxiety— which stayed in a subdued form, throughout that night. Two months later, when he read the book again, he was so well psychologically defended that reading the book was only an academic experience.

Frank will never know where he would have gone had he flowed with the experience rather than making himself anxious. One reason this is difficult for many of us to accept, let alone strive for, is that this irrationality resembles craziness. Going crazy is something most of us fear, even though we all are crazy. Perhaps a better way of saying this is that most of us fear getting in touch with the crazy part of ourself.

18. An Emotional Acceptance of One's Impending Death

The first trait concerned life; this last one, death. It is this last trait, a genuine understanding of our personal death, that makes life itself so meaningful. How could one value life if it lasted forever? What would be worth valuing?

Our culture hides death. Death is considered ugly. People are taken out of their homes to die, and young children are often not permitted to attend funerals. Funerals themselves have evolved into a series of fancy trappings which in themselves mask that which is most feared. All of us know in our heads that some day we will die. Yet most of us really cannot accept this fact, nor are we able to deal with it on a real, gut (emotional) level. Instead, we block our feelings about death. The most violent, yet psychologically rewarding, physical reactions I have ever seen in therapy or sensitivity groups occurred when people (through the use of relaxation and fantasy) have been forced to deal with their own future deaths.

The biggest difference between people and animals is that people are always beings toward a future. Existence includes the future. Both people and animals experience a present, and both experience a past (if not, you would not be able to train animals). But only a human can consider future possibilities. One very important future possibility for all of us is our death. Since I don't think we ever experience our death, another way to consider this is that our dying and the thought of our death is part of our existence. By denying death, on either a personal or cultural level, we also deny an important part of our humanness.

Elizabeth Kubler-Ross's *On Death and Dying* is, in my opinion, probably the most important piece of research done during the past decade in the social sciences. She has given us the insight needed to begin to deal both personally and professionally with the topic of death. I think that this topic will become so important that within ten years, no one will be able to get a college degree in psychology without taking a course on dying and death.

Recently, a person very close to me died of cancer. During the last two months of that person's life, I spent most of my time with her. This experience taught me that being with (emotionally) a dying person was a real threat to my ego, not just because of the loss of a loved one but also because of its reminder of my own finitude. Yet such a reminder is exactly what we all need in order to live life in a fully human way and, when the time comes, die in a fully human manner.

Accepting our death also means accepting the process that leads to that death, namely, aging. Our denial of death is reflected in our denial of the aging process. Too many middle-aged people spend much time and money trying to either be or

at least appear young again. Too many old people are declared useless by their society and made to live out their life in poverty and boredom. How can we let this happen in view of the fact that we all know that unless fate intervenes first, we'll all be there too some day? But do we all know that? In our heads we do, of course, but emotionally (and probably unconsciously, if you believe in such a concept) it is often you and thee, but not me—denial, a lack of acceptance of our own future nonexistence. By confronting the problem of aging, we would also have to confront our own death, and that's scary.

Many other social problems, aside from aging, are directly related to our social-psychological denial of death. Do you think the atom bomb would have ever been invented if those developers really understood that one day they might be under that big white cloud? Do you think the pollution problem would have ever got this bad if people really could accept the fact that one day *they* might not be able to breathe?

Mentally healthy persons can go beyond the life-death dichotomy. They understand that the one gives meaning to the other and that only by accepting the fact that our existence could end at any time will we be able to fully appreciate, value, and enjoy life—now.

> "To be or not to be is not the question;
> For to be is not to be."
>
> Alan Watts (1961, p.115)

* * *

No one reading this book has reached his or her full potential. For that reason, no one is as mentally healthy as he or she can be. *Everyone* has room to grow. This is one of the exciting things about the human condition. If anyone ever reached his or her fullest potential, what would be the purpose of continuing? What would one strive for? The best thing to strive for would then be to stay the same, but that could be very boring.

Who, then, is the mentally healthy person? *It is whoever comes closer than most of us to reaching his or her full potential.* That statement is overworked, and most of you have heard it, or something similar to it, before, but I cannot think of any better way of saying it. It is, however, important to go beyond this general statement and consider exactly what "reaching full potential" means. That is why I have given the 18 traits that I feel people must strive for in order to reach their full potential. I hope I have presented the traits in enough detail that the meaning of each is clear, yet ambiguously enough to allow room for your expansions and modifications. Please remember, as I stated earlier, that I've never seen anyone that has actualized all these traits. If Allison were a real person instead of a myth, I'm sure she would have her own special problems, being so different from most other people in so many ways. Allison was presented only to help describe how some of these traits might appear behaviorally.

It is not important that you agree with the traits given; my hope is that my discussion of these things will help stimulate your own thinking on the subject. From there, I hope that each of you will develop your own model, one that you can use to meansure your own growth and one that may be helpful to you as you influence other people.

Finally, it is important to remember that these specific traits are not independent of one another. Rather, they are very much interrelated and interdependent. Throughout this chapter I have made explicit some of these relationships as I see them. For example, in order to engage in new behaviors (trait 14), one must have the ability to take risks (trait 5). In order to be open to new information coming from within (trait 13), one must be aware of what one's body is saying (trait 12). As you develop your own model, try to map out the possible interactions among the various traits. I think you'll discover that mental health is a self-stimulating process. As one area of a person develops, it stimulates further growth in other areas.

Every aspect of a person is interrelated with every other aspect, because people are more than the sum total of their parts. This "something more" is what makes each person unique, and there is no way to describe what it is. If you have ever experienced an open, deep, meaningful relationship with another person, you know what I am talking about. It is this indescribable thing, which transcends all traits and behaviors, that makes people human and lovable to other people.

Ways of Achieving the Model

Chapter Four

Today, the biggest block to becoming, to growing, is that too many people are complacent about not becoming, not growing toward their fullest potential. Many people feel that there are no alternatives to conforming, normal behaviors other than undesirable behaviors, such as those associated with mental illness. The myth that keeps this belief alive is probably the most damaging of all our many social myths.

Before we consider ways of achieving the model, the question of whether or not we *want* to be mentally healthy must be considered. Unlike physical health, which has almost all positive attributes associated with it, mental health has both positive and negative aspects. For all the positive attributes, there are also many special problems that the mentally healthy person has to deal with. For example, in Chapter Three, Frank was shown to deny contradictions in himself and was therefore usually able to behave in a very predictable manner. This makes a friendship with him in some ways more comfortable than one with Allison, who behaves in less predictable ways. Maslow has observed that the healthy people he studied seemed to have fewer friends than do most people,but that these friendships were usually much deeper, with more sharing between persons and more stimulation toward personal and relationship growth. Being different can sometimes be a very lonely experience.

Another disadvantage of mental health is that if one is continually engaging in new behaviors and taking risks, one can get scared and tired. The security and rest which come from habitual behavior is absent. Of course, also absent is the boredom and lack of personal growth that is associated with habitual behaviors.

Each person must decide whether he or she is ready and willing to suffer growing pains and move forward in life. Along with the pains, however, is an ecstasy that cannot be found in the middle ground of nonmovement. The joy associated with open, meaningful relationships, with getting in touch with our humanness, and with mastering new behaviors is indescribable. It needs to be experienced, not read about, in order to be understood. You are responsible for yourself. Only you can choose whether or not your primary personal goal is to conform or to grow. If your choice is the former, please remember that it is an O.K. choice. It is every bit as valid as the latter possibility. Later in your life, you may change and choose development over adjustment. Some time later, I may change and choose adjustment as my primary goal. Death is the only irreversible choice.

What, then, are some ways to grow, to actualize potentials, if one so chooses? In this chapter, I will present a few ideas for adults, for educational institutions, and for child-rearing practices. Each of these topics is worthy of a lengthy book in and of itself. The discussion in this chapter makes no pretense of completeness, and I hope that this brief discussion will not distract from the major idea I am trying to present in this book—how you can set up goals or models to help yourself see where it is you would like to go in terms of personal growth. Growth is a three-step process. First, determine the goal—what kind of person do you want to become. Second, decide how you can achieve that goal. Third, go out and attempt to achieve the goal, making adjustments in the goal and/or method as you deem necessary or desirable.

This chapter differs from the general topic of this book in that it deals with the second step—how to move toward the already thought-out goal. Details and specifics here are not important, because what I will present relates only to the model of health I developed in Chapter Three. Once you have developed your own model of health, you will need to develop your own process of implementing that model. I present this abbreviated plan for growth not to tell you that this is the way to grow or that this is the way to teach or that this is the way to be a good parent; rather, I hope to demonstrate that the model presented in Chapter Three is not just "pie in the sky." I would like to show that once a model of mental health is developed, it can become an action plan and put to practical use—not just condemned to the realm of an academic exercise.

1. For Adults

You learn the most about yourself and about your environment when you engage in new behaviors. Seeing how you feel about yourself and seeing how others respond to you when you do different things is one way to get data about yourself, data from which you can learn and grow. This is especially true when the new behaviors involve interpersonal interactions, for we get most of our information about our selfhood from relations with other people. The best way for you to grow as an individual (and for your relationships to grow as relationships) is to take some risks and continually explore new and different areas of the relationship. Hopefully, these new behaviors can be meaningful in that they will be progressing toward a more genuine expression of feelings. The next time you are with someone you feel like touching, reach out. See what happens. The next time you get angry with a friend, express it. See what it does to the relationship. I think most of you will be pleasantly surprised at your own ability to take risks and at the positive results for both you and the relationship.

For me, the key word is "risk." I find it important to not only engage in new behaviors, but also confront those situations which scare me the most. I grow when I find out what is making me afraid. I also usually lose the fear when I go ahead and engage in the feared behavior, because things usually don't turn out as badly as I imagined they would. Risk-taking is a very individualized concept because, what is scary for one person may be a very comfortable experience for someone else. For example, I have trouble being quiet in a crowd. When I am my usual assertive, aggressive self, I can be fairly sure about how people will respond to me. But the risk for me is being quiet with people. Will I still be recognized? Will I still exist? You, however, may find it easy to be quiet. For you, being assertive, giving your opinions, etc., may be a high-risk thing because being quiet is your usual mode of behavior. The nature of the risk is a very individualized thing and can be judged only by the person involved, not by an outsider just looking at the behavior.

Risk-taking is not an all-or-none situation. Everyone takes risks occasionally, and even the bravest person doesn't always do what he or she thinks best. We are continually confronted with new situations in which we must choose either growth or safety—to tell or not to tell someone your feeling of love, to tell or not to tell someone you are angry, to take a course from a stimulating teacher or an easy teacher. Growth is directly related to the formula

$$\frac{\text{No. of growth choices}}{\text{No. of safety choices}}$$

and only you know the score!

So far, I have talked about an individual either reaching out alone or being lucky enough to have a friend who takes the initiative in order to break habitual ways of relating to others. There are other ways that you, as adults, can work to actualize your own potentials in the area of mental health. One way is through disciplined use of your powers of reflection, which means thinking about your lived experiences—trying to grasp what you are doing in the world and how you are doing it. The stated purpose of this book is to try to encourage you to reflect, in a structured and detailed way, on the meaning the concepts of health and normalcy have for your life.

The most helpful tool I have found for stimulating growth toward mental health is the therapeutic process, a situation in which a trained person helps other individuals to grow. This therapeutic process includes traditional individual and group therapy, as well as the groups associated with the "human potential movement" (sensitivity groups, encounter groups, T-groups, etc.). This process is only a technical device intended to facilitate growth. People can grow without it—very few people *need* it; however, it is a helpful aid. I think that if people fully understood this concept, some of the negative social connotations associated with therapy would dissipate.

The same reason that makes this process important in growth toward actualization is also a valid criticism of the technique as it is traditionally used. It seems to work best for those who need it the least. For someone out of touch with reality, the process is just about useless. For a moderately troubled person who goes to a therapist once or twice a week, it often works reasonably well. For the "average" person, who goes for the purpose of actualizing more of his or her potentials (becoming mentally healthier), the process often works very well. Rather than seeking individual help, a large portion of the latter group go to encounter-type groups, including sensitivity groups. Carl Rogers, a well-known psychologist, has called the encounter movement the most important social invention of our time. It certainly has been one of the most significant things in my life. It was in such a group that I discovered that I could be different from average, and a number of such group experiences helped me to develop the confidence and tools for growing, both inside and outside of groups.

It is difficult for me to describe encounter groups, because the essence of these groups is in the participants' personal involvement in the group process. However, if you would like to read, in some detail, about groups, I would suggest two books by Schutz: *Joy* and *Here Comes Everybody,* the latter being the best-written description of group work I have ever read.

Many of the people who ask me for books to read on this subject and who then want to talk about them do not have the courage to join a group. It is a risk they are not ready to take.

But when you stand around a circle at the end of a week-end marathon group, with your arms around people you feel very close to, feeling very in touch with yourself, singing "Bridge Over Troubled Water," with your heart dancing like the flicker of a candle's flame, then you understand what a group is about, and you understand better what you're about.

The professional journals in psychology have reported a number of studies which demonstrate that encounter-type groups do help people develop some of the traits listed in Chapter Three. It is not my intent to review the professional literature, but I do want to cite one example to help explain how I think groups are functional in helping people to develop mental health. For a long time, self-esteem was considered to be a fairly stable personality trait. Once it was formed, it was fairly resistant to change. Recently, there have been a number of studies which have shown that self-esteem increases in people who have participated in groups. Self-esteem is not only an important trait in itself, but it also relates to other positive traits (ability to give and receive love, high risk-taking, etc.). Why would a group help someone develop self-esteem? First, we all have some bad feelings about ourselves; we do not usually share these feelings with others, and others do not share with us their bad feelings about themselves. When others do open themselves to us, however, we realize that the "bad" things we were hiding are often common to other people as well as that they are not so uniquely bad after all. The second reason was best described by my closest friend (my wife) after a group experience. She said, "I revealed all those 'bad' things about myself, and yet those people still liked me. Maybe I'm not so bad after all."

The emphasis in this discussion may seem overweighted toward some of the negative aspects of selfhood (revealing "hidden" or "bad" traits about oneself) and thus incongruent with my experiences in groups. Unfortunately, this emphasis can become verification for many of the misconceptions that already exist concerning these groups. Too often, when the idea of open, honest communication is discussed, people assume that if someone talks honestly to them, it will be mostly an exercise in hearing negative reactions. What seems unconsidered is that it is a real risk to say to someone "I really like you and would like to be your friend" or "You are a beautiful person." When you hear honest communication occurring, positive expressions usually far outnumber negative ones. One of the nicest outcomes for me in terms of my group participation has been a reinforcement of my optimistic view of human beings. I am convinced that when we go beyond the surface differences that separate us (black-white, male-female, liberal-conservative, introvert-extrovert, young-old, student-worker) and explore some of our common humanness, we will find that we basically like one another, can express that liking, and can use that expression as a basis for mutual support.

2. In Educational Practices

From kindergarten to college our educational system is marked by rigidity and closedness. By rigid I mean that the goals and methods of education today are not that much different from those of 25 years ago, even though the world is much, much different today. We are still training people for jobs that do not exist. As an example, consider how many certified teachers can't find a job today. Nonetheless, schools of education still accept and train a high percentage of the student body. Among other things, this rigidity is creating a class of highly educated unemployable persons.

By closedness, I mean that those who run the schools (teachers and administrators) are products of the same system, thus making change difficult. For example, instead of thinking about changing an entire system, look at the problem of changing just a single college classroom. It is usually a waste of time for a student to tell a teacher that multiple-choice exams are absurd because they force students to spend more time in memorizing than in thinking. After all, the teacher is the teacher only because he or she was good at taking multiple-choice exams. It's unfair and unrealistic to expect many advanced-degree people to repudiate their backgrounds, from which they derive much of their esteem and prestige.

However, individual teachers at any level can have an important impact and can be a stimulus for growth toward mental health for some of their students. If nothing else, an "abnormal" teacher can at least slow down the school's attempt to destroy the potential growth of its students. But although the schools don't help people reach their fullest potential, they do help persuade millions of persons that normalcy is desirable. In short, this is the job the educational system was intended to do, and at this the schools have succeeded.

Schools are not failures because they don't help promote full growth. The job of schools in any society with mass education is not to produce great people, but rather to socialize the young generation—to make them normal, average, predictable, and somewhat controllable. Schools are a tremendous success. The possibility of individual teachers' making significant changes within this successful system is a complicated issue and well beyond the scope of this text. (If you would like to read further on this topic, see the book by W. Postman and C. Weingartner, *Teaching As A Subversive Activity*.) But it should at least be noted that teachers choosing to work toward the goal of enhancing students' mental health will often find themselves in a lonely position, unsupported by authority, and often risking their advancement or even the job itself.

Listed below are six of the mental-health traits discussed in Chapter Three, with brief suggestions about how a teacher might help children actualize these potentials. Although none of these ideas is especially unusual, implementing these ideas is still the exception rather than the rule in most schools.

A. *Time Competence*

School is basically future-oriented. The training is for the future, and the rewards (except for a gold star or an "A" here and there) are in the future. But it is possible for school to be more present-oriented. If students do not enjoy attending school, we ought to find out why and explore what we can do about it rather than saying, "Well, it's always been that way." The material taught ought to be of interest to the students. For example, history can be taught in such a way that the Vietnam war and the American Civil War are related. The French Revolution can be complared to the urban riots of the 1960s in America. Subtraction can be taught as the difference between the number of runs scored last night by John's and Bob's Little League teams. In short, almost anything taught can be related to the meaningful, everyday experience of the student; lessons need not be abstract, uninteresting, or "academic." Teachers can talk to students about what they are doing today, their attitude emphasizing that today is important and that childhood is more than a preparation for adult life—that it is life itself.

B. *Internal Locus of Validation and Motivation*

In most school situations the teacher tells students how and what to study and then proceeds to evaluate them on how well they did it. How can we ever expect students to evaluate themselves if we teachers are forever putting grades on everything they do? What do you think would happen if teachers refused to tell students how and what to study, refused to evaluate them, and instead presented themselves as a resource for the students to use in the ways they saw fit? Carl Rogers' book *Freedom to Learn* describes such a situation. At the beginning, students had to work through their frustration, but the end result was that some very valuable personal, as well as academic, learning took place.

C. High Risk-taking Behavior

School could be a place in which students risk making mistakes in order to learn. Early in their school career, children learn that mistakes in school mean that they are either dumb or unprepared, both of which result in negative evaluations by the teacher. How absurd to have a test at the end of a unit, when it is time to move on to something else; rather, the test could be used as a feedback mechanism to help both the student and the teacher discover what material needs to be gone over again. Again, the attitude of the teacher is most important here.

D. Authentic Communication

The best way to encourage authentic communication is to model that type of behavior with the students. Teachers can express anger, joy, and all other emotions without losing the "respect" of their students. The concepts of professional role and distance are usually only excuses not to be open and honest.

E. Taking Responsibility for Oneself

Teachers can present to students the idea that there is no such thing as objectivity divorced from the experiencing person. Anything perceived, thought about, and spoken is partly a reflection of the perceiver, thinker, or speaker. All academic data, then, can also be seen as personal data. Students can be encouraged to use a language that indicates and reaffirms the understanding of their partial responsibility for a given event. Students can begin to say, "The meaning I give to this situation" rather than "This is the way it is."

In my own college classes at the beginning of each semester, I set up communication rules or guidelines. I explain that teaching and learning are experiences in communication and that the better we communicate, the better and the more efficient the classroom. Among the guidelines are: (1) Always use the pronoun "I" when speaking about yourself. Don't disguise your feelings behind such impersonal pronouns as "people feel that that . . . ," etc. If the class agrees with someone's statement, we can yell "right on," and then we'll understand that the statement can be generalized. Until then, however, students can speak for only themselves. (2) Avoid controlling words, e.g., "have to," and ambiguous words, e.g., "should." Instead, explain what you mean. (3) Whenever you want to ask a question, first consider whether there is a statement behind the question. Instead of saying "Could you explain more about point x?" say "That was a dumb statement you just made, teacher." We can respond to one another's statements easier than we can to questions with hidden meanings and messages. Also, students can be encouraged to recognize their freedom of choice, so that they begin to understand and express the idea that the completed homework assignment is one that they *chose* to complete (given the situation) as opposed to one that they *had* to complete.

F. Accepts Contradictions in Self

I think that people would be able to deal more easily with their own complexities and contradictions if cultural heroes were also seen as the complex individuals that they are. Schools generally present historical characters in such a superficial, simple way that students come to assume that these people really were simple to understand—undirectional (all good) persons. For example, Franklin Roosevelt is generally considered as a great American, an independent leader with a great concern for people. Although this might be basically true, Roosevelt also had great dependency needs (directed particularly toward his mother) and once reacted to a complex political and economic situation by sending a boatload of German Jews back to Hitler's Germany. In short, he (as is everyone else) was a very complex man with many contradictions, motives, needs, and behaviors. It seems to me that if these things were emphasized more in schools, children would be better able to accept their own complexity, which is the essence of their humanness.

* * *

The specific traits mentioned here are not the important issue. What is important is that you consider your own model of mental health and then examine how your behavior relates to that model. In that way, your teaching behavior can be made more meaningful and more goal-directed, less random, static, or rigid.

3. In Child-rearing Practices

It seems to me that the most important aspect of child-rearing practices is the attitude of the parents. Their attitude must convey to the child that he or she is a worthy person, is loved, that life is worth living, and that there is some order to life. Parents must convey to the child that what they do as parents, both the prohibitions and the permissions, has some meaning and that this meaning is in the interest of both the child and society. This attitude is conveyed not by the quantity of things (the amount of of food a child gets, the number of times the parents say "I love you"), but rather by the general, overall quality of the parent-child relationship. (A more detailed discussion of this is presented in Erik Erikson's *Childhood and Society*.)

In terms of specific parental behaviors, my thinking has been greatly influenced by the work of Stanley Coopersmith (*Antecedents of Self-Esteem*). His research suggests that there are three factors which are helpful in developing high self-esteem in a child: (1) Complete and total acceptance and love by the parents. This, of course, either is or is not present. There does not seem to be much that can be done if this is missing; (2) Limits set for the child; (3) Freedom within these limits. It is this combination of freedom and limits that seems to give many parents trouble. Theoretically, it seems easier to take one side or the other, to be either permissive or restrictive. Although freedom within limits seems to be a difficult task, in my opinion it works best for the child in the long run. For example, suppose that a seven-year-old's parents have decided that the child has to be in bed at a certain time and must take a bath before going to bed. Within these limits, it should then be up to the child, not the parents, to decide how to schedule things so that the bath is out of the way by the time it's bedtime.

Children learn by doing. The more freedom a child has to do things (within reasonable limits), the more the child will learn, and the greater the child's confidence will be in his or her ability to master the world. This means that it is essential for children to do things for themselves. The child's frustration of not getting something done is small compared to the good feelings he or she gets from accomplishing something. Exploring one's world means making a mess. Few things are as damaging to a child's growth as a mother's need for a tidy house.

How a parent deals with the child's emotions is also a very important factor in the child's development (as well as that of the parent). If emotions, e.g., anger, are labeled as bad, it makes it harder for children to deal with them. The same is true for different behaviors. If a young child's sexual behavior, e.g., playing "doctor," is associated with a strong, negative parental reaction, it is possible that the child will have problems in this area later in life. The best thing a parent can do is relax and let the child express a wide range of feelings and behaviors. If anything seems to extreme or unusual, the parents can seek guidance from a professional.

It is also important for parents to be open with their children. Children are egocentric. If a parent is obviously upset but is not talking about it, most children will assume that the parent is angry at them, when in fact it is just as likely that the parent has just had a disagreement with someone else. "Sparing" children from your problems and worries does not usually turn out to be a favor to them.

Finally, I think that it is very important that parents get as much away from traditional sex roles as possible. If a boy has to "act like a man" and not cry if he gets hurt and if a girl is raised with the dream of being a nurse rather than a doctor, neither will grow up with the full range of human potentials open to them. Studies have shown that creative children are both sensitive and independent. We teach boys to be independent, but not sensitive; we teach girls to be sensitive, but not independent. Therefore, most creative potential in our culture is killed by bringing children up to be ladies and gentlemen rather than just people. The children who become creative anyway often pay a big price for their creativeness. They are different from most other children, and clinical studies have shown they are often lonely and unhappy. Hopefully, this will change as the negative aspects of traditional roles become better known.

. . . Or Not to be a Clangbird

Chapter Five

From reading this book, you can easily get the idea that I am saying that being normal is not good. It is not a question of good or bad. Rather, the point of this book is to try to show that in the mental-health area, there is a deviation from normalcy in a direction other than pathology. Maybe we as teachers and future teachers, social scientitsts and future social scientists, parents and future parents, and citizens owe it to the next generation to consider a mental-health model—not just a conforming, normal-person model—as the basis for our strategies in planning educational directions, social and political action, and child-rearing. Maybe we owe it to ourselves to consider this kind of model in living our own lives today—for we are, too.

Children come into the world curious and interested in almost everything around them. Within the first year of life, they become aware of their body, aware that it belongs to them, and they delight in this awareness. Then, something happens to most of us. As we grow older, we decrease our areas of interest. (One socially acceptable term for adults is specialization.) At the same time, we become less and less aware of ourselves, our needs, and even our physical properties. Most of us end up like the mythical clangbird:

> The clangbird is a huge mechanical monster which soars high in the heavens above in ever-decreasing concentric circles until it flies up its own asshole and, with a loud, resounding clang, its existence ends.

You can be the clangbird or you can be Allison. You have the freedom to choose (B. F. Skinner lied to you!). Until you are ready to choose to grow (not to choose is to choose not to)—until you are ready, at the gut level, to take some risks—be careful where you fly!

Bibliography

Listed here are some of the works that have had a major influence on my thinking about the topic of mental health. Some of these references are directly referred to and quoted in this book. This reading list may be a good starting point for anyone who would like to further consider the concept of mental health. Some of the writers, such as Abraham Maslow and Carl Rogers, have written so much that I have listed only those works which have had the greatest influence on me. Each book cited contains a reference list; you may want to use these references in addition to, or instead of, the ones cited here .

Bach, Richard. *Jonathan Livingston Seagull*, New York: MacMillan, 1970.

Berne, Eric. *Games People Play*, New York: Grove Press, 1964.

Castaneda, Carlos. *A Separate Reality*, New York: Simon & Schuster, 1971.

Coopersmith, Stanley. *The Antecedents of Self-Esteem*, San Francisco: W. H. Freeman, 1967.

Dumont, Matthew. *The Absurd Healer: Perspectives of a Community Psychiatrist*, New York: Science House, 1968.

Erikson, Erik. *Childhood and Society*, New York: W. W. Norton, 1950.

Exupery, Antoine de Saint. *The Little Prince*, New York: Harcourt, Brace and World, 1943.

Farber, Jerry. *The Student as Nigger*, New York: Pocket Books, 1970.

Frankl, Viktor. *Man's Search for Meaning*, New York: Pocket Books, 1959.

Fromm, Erich. *Man For Himself*, New York: Fawcett, 1947.

——. *The Art of Loving*, New York: Bantam Books, 1956.

Gardner, John. *Self-Renewal*, New York: Harper & Row, 1963.

Gibran, Kahlil. *The Prophet*, New York: Knopf, 1923.

——' *A Tear and a Smile*, New York: Knopf, 1950.

Giorgi, Amedeo. *Psychology as a Human Science: A Phenomenologically Based Approach*, New York: Harper & Row, 1970.

Haley, Jay. *The Power Tactics of Jesus Christ*, New York: The Hearst Corporation, 1969.

James, Muriel and Dorothy Jongeward. *Born to Win: Transactional Analysis with Gestalt Experiments,* Reading, Mass.: Addison-Wesley, 1971.

Jourard, Sidney. *Self-Disclosure: An Experimental Analysis of the Transparent Self*, New York: Wiley, 1971.

Kaufmann, Walter. *The Protable Nietzsche*, New York: The Viking Press, 1954.

Keen, Ernest. *Psychology and the New Consciousness,* Monterey, Cal.: Brooks/Cole, 1972.

Keyes, Charles. *God or Ichabod?* Cincinnati, Ohio: Forward Movement, 1973.

Kozol, Jonathan. *Death at an Early Age*, New York: Bantam, 1967.

Kubler-Ross, Elizabeth. *On Death and Dying*, New York: MacMillian, 1969.

Laing, R. D. *The Politics of Experience*, New York: Ballantine Books, 1967.

——. *Knots,* New York: Pantheon Books, 1970.

Lederman, Janet. *Anger and the Rocking Chair: Gestalt Awareness with Children*, New York: McGraw-Hill, 1969.

Leifer, Ronald. *In the Name of Mental Health: The Social Functions of Psychiatry,* New York: Science House, 1969.

Maslow, A. H. *Motivation and Personality,* New York: Harper & Row, 1954.

——. *Towards a Psychology of Being,* New York: Van Nostrand Reinhold, 1962.

——. *The Farther Reaches of Human Nature*, New York: The Viking Press, 1971.

May, Rollo. *Love and Will,* New York: Norton, 1969.

——. Ernest Angle and Heri Ellenberger, eds. *Existence*, New York: Simon & Schuster, 1958.

Mead, Margaret. *Culture and Commitment,* New York: The American Museum of Natural History, 1970.

O'Neal, N. and G. O'Neal. *Open Marriage,* New York: Evans, 1972.

Perls, Frederick. *In and Out of the Garbage Pail,* Lafayett, Cal.: The Real People Press, 1967.

Postman, N. and C. Weingartner. *Teaching as a Subversive Activity,* New York: Dell, 1969.

Rogers, Carl R. *On Becoming a Person,* Boston: Houghton Mifflin, 1961.

——. *Freedom to Learn*, Columbus, Ohio: Charles E. Merrill, 1969.

Schutz, William. *Joy: Expanding Human Awareness,* New York: Grove Press, 1967.

——. *Here Comes Everybody,* New York: Harper & Row, 1971.

Shostrom, Everett. *Man, the Manipulator,* New York: Bantam Books, 1968.

Stewart, John, ed. *Bridges not Walls,* Reading, Mass.: Addison-Wesley, 1973.

Torbet, Dave. *Three of a Kind,* Boise, Idaho: Boise State College Press, 1968.

van den Berg, J. H. *A Different Existence,* Pittsburgh, Pa.: Duquesne University Press, 1972.

Watts, Alan. *Psychotherapy East and West,* New York: Ballantine Books, 1961.

——. *The Book: On the Taboo Against Knowing Who You Are,* New York: Collier Books, 1969.